Really Ridiculous
Rabbit Riddles

By Jeanne &
Margaret Wallace
and Dave Ross

pictures by Dave Ross

SCHOLASTIC INC.
New York Toronto London Auckland Sydney Tokyo

ISBN 0-590-05764-2

15 14 13 12 11 10 9 8 7 6 5   4 5 6 7 8/8

Printed in the U.S.A.   07

Where do you find rabbits?

It depends on where they were lost.

How do you catch a rabbit?

Hide behind a tree and make a noise like a carrot.

What did the rabbit say to the carrot?

It's been nice gnawing you.

What do rabbits have that no other animal has?

Baby rabbits.

When is it proper to drink rabbit's milk?

When you are a baby rabbit.

Where was the rabbit when the lights went out?

In the dark.

What should you do with a rabbit who is eating a dictionary?

Take the words right out of his mouth.

Why don't rabbits play football?

Their ears won't fit in the helmets.

How can you tell if a 500 pound rabbit is under your bed?

You can touch the ceiling with your nose.

Why didn't Joe put an ad in the paper when he lost his rabbit?

Joe's rabbit never reads the paper.

Why was the rabbit in the Westinghouse refrigerator?

He was westing.

ow do you know when you have 200 rabbits in your refrigerator?

The door won't shut.

How long should a rabbit's legs be?

Long enough to reach the ground.

Why don't rabbits ride tricycles?

They don't have a thumb to ring the bell.

What is sadder than a giraffe with a sore throat

A rabbit with an earache.

What is the rabbit's favorite dance?

The bunny hop.

The more he takes away the bigger it becomes.
What is it?

A rabbit hole.

What would you call a cold puppy sitting on a rabbit?

A chili dog on a bun.

What is a rabbit after it's four days old?

Five days old.

What would you get if you threw a white rabbit in the Red Sea?

A wet rabbit.

What is the difference between a crazy rabbit and a counterfeit quarter?

LIBERTY

1978

One is a mad bunny and the other is bad money.

What would you call a rabbit who is mad at the sun?

A hot cross bunny.

What can a rabbit do that an elephant can't?

Hide in a bucket.

What would you get if you crossed a rabbit with a bumblebee?

A honey bunny.

What do you call a rabbit comedian?

A funny bunny.

What would you get if you crossed a rabbit with an insect?

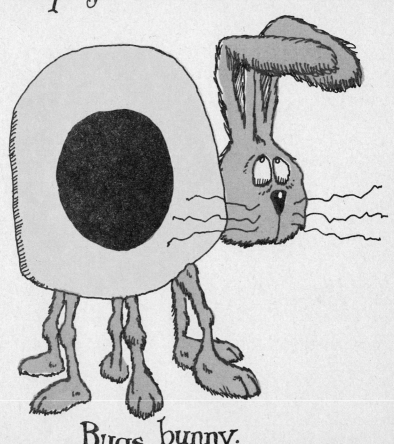

Bugs bunny.

What would you have if you ate nothing but carrots?

A rabbit habit

How many dumb bunnies does it take to change a lightbulb?

Three. One to hold the bulb and two to turn the ladder.

Why is a leaky faucet like a cowardly bunny?

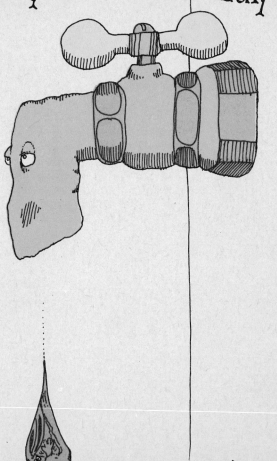

Because it runs.

Why is a rabbit like a dime?

Because it has a head on one end and a tail on the other.

Why do rabbits have shiny noses?

Because the powder puff is at the wrong end

What kind of an umbrella does a rabbit carry on a rainy day?

A wet one.

How many rabbits can you put in an empty cage?

Only one. After that it's not empty.

What has a fluffy tail, four legs, and wings?

A rabbit with a canary on his head.